NORMAN VINCENT PEALE

Words I Have Lived By

from "My Favorite Quotations"

The C.R. Gibson Company · Norwalk, Connecticut 06856

Contents

Introduction

*W*inston Churchill once said, "It is a good thing to read books of quotations. The quotations when engraved upon the memory give you good thoughts."

And to have "good thoughts" is important, for a person becomes what he thinks. Gautama Buddha told us that. "Mind is everything," he said. "We become what we think."

Charles Edison, one-time governor of New Jersey and son of the famous inventor Thomas A. Edison, was a personal friend of mine; I was with him many times. He loved to talk about his father and told me many stories about him.

It seems that the older Edison thought that the mind is our greatest asset and would often say to his son, "The primary function of the body is to carry the brain." That is not a direct quotation, being simply a remark in conversation, but it may be taken to represent the inventor's thinking. The brain, besides directing motor activity, is, of course, the instrument by which one remembers, considers, evaluates, thinks. And it is through the wonders of the brain that one knows God, the Creator of it all.

William James, sometimes called the father of American psychological science, expressed agreement with these ideas and went even further: "The greatest discovery of my generation is that human beings can alter their lives by altering their attitudes of mind." Professor James's generation lived in what may be called an age of discovery. During that era some of the most notable discoveries of science took place. But the supreme discovery is that we can change our lives by the changing of mental attitudes.

That being true—and that it is true is a generally accepted fact today—then anything that can contribute to a thought process that changes our basic attitudes is of value. I have found over many years that the habit of dropping choice thoughts into consciousness and allowing them to permeate the mental structure results finally in a thought pattern that affects virtually the totality of one's life.

The quotation just cited from William James, for example, was dropped into my thoughts one day long ago as I sat in class at Boston University. It was as if I had been hit by a bolt of lightning. It struck me so forcibly that it vitally affected my total thinking. The truth of it seemed certain. I believed it; I accepted it. From my background, I associated personal change with faith and, in a flash of insight, knew that I could change my life by changing my attitudes of mind. I've been advocating that truth about people ever since.

So the object of this book of quotations is to bring to readers the thoughts I have picked up in a lifetime of reading, as well as others heard in conversation with all sorts of people. All wisdom is not in the past. But, when working with quotations, an old saying often comes to mind: "There is nothing new under the sun." Often today's speakers, writers, and conversationalists may come up with a new formulation of an ancient truth that is fascinating, even exciting. We may expect that these truths may continue to be quoted 100 years from now, perhaps modernized to fit the late twenty-first century.

I have had a lot of pleasure in gathering together these favorite quotations. Incidents in which the quotations have been meaningful to me have come to mind as I collected them for this book. I could actually make another book of stories about those incidents. But for now, just read a few of these quotations at a time and let them "germinate," shall we say, in your consciousness. They may start something. And, when engraved upon the memory, as Churchill said, they will indeed "give you good thoughts."

I hope that you have as much pleasure in reading them as I did when putting them together in this book. And may I add perhaps the greatest quotation of all, though I do not know who first said it: "God bless you."

Norman Vincent Peale

·One·

Daily Life and Work

$\mathcal{A}$ s I write this, autumn has returned to the Northeast where I live, and the hills and valleys are bathed in the special light that gives the landscape a crystal clarity.

Vacations are over, and most of us are busy with our work. For some, unfortunately, the daily routine is drudgery; the surveys say that millions of people hate their jobs. But it need not be so! For decades, I have been saying that an enthusiastic, positive outlook can transform any situation, and thousands of individuals testify to the truth of that claim.

It used to be stated—perhaps sometimes with justification—that religion was a matter of "pie in the sky by and by." But real religion is and always has been redemption in the here-and-now as well as a strongly based hope for the hereafter. The realities of faith, hope, and love can make every day an exciting adventure.

I contend that how you do something and the attitude with which you do it are usually even more important than what you do. The other day a friend remarked, "I just had a good, long walk to the post office, and I made an important discovery." When I asked him what he discovered, he said, "During the fall and winter, I try to get as much sun as possible. On my walk today, I could have been in the shade most of the time, and I found it was just as easy to walk on the sunny side of the street."

Often we have no choice about doing things, but we can always choose how to do them. And that, as the following quotations illustrate, can make all the difference in your daily life.

The greatest use of life is to spend it for something that will outlast it.

William James

Opportunity is missed by most people because it is dressed in overalls and looks like work.

Thomas A. Edison

Work! Thank God for the swing of it, for the clamoring, hammering ring of it.

Angela Morgan

Diligence is the mother of good luck, and God gives all things to industry.

Benjamin Franklin

Strong lives are motivated by dynamic purposes.

Kenneth Hildebrand

Art is right reason in the doing of work.

St. Thomas Aquinas

When the going gets tough, let the tough get going.

Frank Leahy

Turn your stumbling blocks into stepping stones.

Anonymous

Always take an emergency leisurely.

Chinese Proverb

We have a problem. "Congratulations." But it's a tough problem. "Then double congratulations."

W. Clement Stone

Men are born to succeed, not to fail.

Henry David Thoreau

Choose your rut carefully; you'll be in it for the next ten miles.

Road Sign in Upstate New York

If at first you don't succeed, try, try again.

William Edward Hickson

Never despair, but if you do, work on in despair.

Edmund Burke

It is a funny thing about life; if you refuse to accept anything but the best, you very often get it.

W. Somerset Maugham

Problems are only opportunities in work clothes.

Henry J. Kaiser

When the rock is hard, we get harder than the rock. When the job is tough, we get tougher than the job.

George Cullum, Sr.

To every disadvantage there is a corresponding advantage.

W. Clement Stone

In adversity remember to keep an even mind.

Horace

There is no sense in the struggle, but there is no choice but to struggle.

Ernie Pyle

We are so outnumbered there's only one thing to do. We must attack.

Sir Andrew Cunningham

Strong people are made by opposition like kites that go up against the wind.

Frank Harris

It is a rough road that leads to the heights of greatness.

Lucius Annaeus Seneca

In our day, when a pitcher got into trouble in a game, instead of taking him out, our manager would leave him in and tell him to pitch his way out of trouble.

Cy (Denton True) Young

Grant me the courage not to give up even though I think it is hopeless.

Chester W. Nimitz

In all human affairs there are *efforts,* and there are *results,* and the strength of the effort is the measure of the result.

James Allen

I would never have amounted to anything were it not for adversity. I was forced to come up the hard way.

J.C.Penney

Those who aim at great deeds must also suffer greatly.

Plutarch

One today is worth two tomorrows; never leave that till tomorrow which you can do today.

Benjamin Franklin

The life given us by nature is short, but the memory of a well-spent life is eternal.

Marcus Tullius Cicero

Still achieving, still pursuing, learn to labor and to wait.

Henry Wadsworth Longfellow

Truth has no special time of its own. Its hour is now—always.

Albert Schweitzer

The heights by great men reached and kept
Were not attained by sudden flight,
But they, while their companions slept,
Were toiling upward in the night.

Henry Wadsworth Longfellow

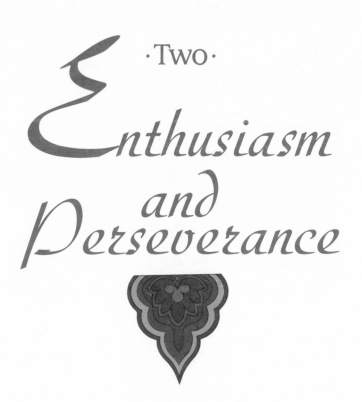

·Two·
Enthusiasm and Perseverance

*S*omewhere out of the past comes a story about three men helping build a cathedral. A passerby, watching one man digging at a wall for the foundation, asked him what he was doing. Between shovels full of earth he grunted, "I'm digging a hole."

A stonemason, asked the same question, answered, "Can't you see I'm making a wall?"

Another laborer was pushing a cart loaded with stones toward the construction site. When he was asked the question, his face lighted up with enthusiasm. He replied, "I'm building a cathedral."

Success at anything requires two vital ingredients: enthusiasm and perseverance. Both can be helped by the broad view that looks beyond temporary difficulties and disappointments to a great goal. What are you doing with your life? Are you putting in time building something lasting and worthwhile? These are questions we must ask ourselves.

Enthusiasm is the priceless quality that makes everything different. The men and women who achieve the most are invariably inspired by enthusiasm. They approach life, its opportunities, and its problems with this vital characteristic.

Successful individuals also keep at it. Great ideas come to naught unless they are carried to completion. When Glenn Cunningham was seven years old, he was so badly burned in a schoolhouse fire that his doctor said, "I doubt if he'll be able to walk again." But the little boy had been motivated by his father to become a champion runner. He visualized himself winning races. Despite intense pain, he struggled to walk again, then to run, although all he could manage at first was a queer hippety-hop gait. But he kept running until he became the outstanding miler of his time.

As you cultivate enthusiasm and perseverance, more power to you!

Enthusiasm is a kind of faith that has been set afire.

George Matthew Adams

I prefer the folly of enthusiasm to the indifference of wisdom.

Anatole France

The real secret of success is enthusiasm. Yes, more than enthusiasm, I would say excitement. I like to see men get excited. When they get excited they make a success of their lives.

Walter Chrysler

I want this team to win. I'm obsessed with winning, with discipline, with achieving.

George Steinbrenner

They never told me I couldn't.

Tom Dempsey

An enthusiast may bore others, but he has never a dull moment himself.

John Kieran

Flaming enthusiasm, backed up by horse sense and persistence, is the quality that most frequently makes for success.

Dale Carnegie

I rate enthusiasm even above professional skill.

Sir Edward Appleton

My mother said to me, "If you become a soldier you'll be a general; if you become a monk you'll end up as the pope." Instead, I became a painter and wound up as Picasso.

Pablo Picasso

He did it with all his heart, and prospered.

2 Chronicles 31:21

One can never consent to creep when one feels an impulse to soar.

Helen Keller

Whatever you do, put romance and enthusiasm into the life of our children.

Margaret Ramsey MacDonald

Act as if it were impossible to fail.

Dorothea Brande

Never, never, never, never give up.

Winston Churchill

And whatsoever ye do, do it heartily.

Colossians 3:23

Don't wait for your ship to come; swim out to it.

Anonymous

Shoot for the moon. Even if you miss it you will land among the stars.

Les Brown

Take calculated risks. That is quite different from being rash.

George S. Patton

The world is moving so fast these days that the man who

says it can't be done is generally interrupted by someone doing it.

Harry Emerson Fosdick

Trifles make perfection, but perfection is no trifle.

Michelangelo

Victory is not won in miles but in inches. Win a little now, hold your ground, and later win a little more.

Louis L'Amour

Wisely, and slow; they stumble that run fast.

William Shakespeare

Perseverance is a great element of success. If you only knock long enough and loud enough at the gate, you are sure to wake up somebody.

Henry Wadsworth Longfellow

Circumstances—what are circumstances? I make circumstances.

Napoleon Bonaparte

The thing always happens that you really believe in; and the belief in a thing makes it happen.

Frank Lloyd Wright

God loves to help him who strives to help himself.

Aeschylus

If a door slams shut it means that God is pointing to an open door further on down.

Anna DeLaney Peale

He that can have patience can have what he will.

Benjamin Franklin

He was a *how* thinker, not an *if* thinker.

Anonymous

We are not creatures of circumstance; we are creators of circumstance.

Benjamin Disraeli

Every noble work is at first impossible.

Thomas Carlyle

Every problem contains the seeds of its own solution.

Stanley Arnold

There ain't nothing from the outside can lick any of us.

Margaret Mitchell in Gone with the Wind

We must dare, and dare again, and go on daring.

George Jacques Danton

The great man is he who does not lose his child's heart.

Mencius

If we really want to live, we'd better start at once to try.

W. H. Auden

·Three·

God's Creation

*O*ne of the happiest men I ever knew was Bill Stidger, a professor, preacher, and writer. He always seemed to be bubbling over with joy and enthusiasm. I remember having some oyster stew with him in the South Station, Boston, and asking him why he was so full of happiness.

He told me that it was because he practiced the attitude of gratitude. "When I wake up in the morning," he said, "I thank the Lord for a sound night's sleep. I give thanks for my wife and children, for the work I have to do, for my friends and opportunities. I just run over the world in my mind, thanking him for the wonderful things in it."

I guarantee that no one can be dull or blasé with such an attitude. And what marvelous things there are for which to be grateful in God's great Creation! My wife, Ruth, and I like to travel. I experience a kind of rebirth every time I think about some of the fascinating places we have visited: Japan with its vibrant aliveness; the green island of Formosa lying in the azure sea; the Philippines and the golden sunlight there; the profound serenity of the great forests of Australia; the breathtaking grandeur of the Swiss mountains; the lovable charm of England; and the beautiful vastness of America, from New England to the Deep South, the Grand Canyon, Alaska, and the matchless Hawaiian Islands.

But above all I am thankful for people like you, the reader of this book, for you are a creation of God unequaled anywhere in the universe. God never made anyone else exactly like you, and he never will again. Thank him for yourself and then for all the rest of his glorious handiwork.

We are his workmanship.

Ephesians 2:10

It's a beautiful day for it.

Daily comment of Wilbur Cross

A sense of curiosity is nature's original school of education.

Smiley Blanton, M.D.

The gathering orange stain
Upon the edge of yonder western peak
Reflects the sunsets of a thousand years.

Anonymous

The sky is the daily bread of the eyes.

Ralph Waldo Emerson

O Lord, how manifold are thy works! in wisdom hast thou
made them all.

Psalm 104:24

Poems are made by fools like me,
But only God can make a tree.

Joyce Kilmer

⚘

I must go down to the seas again,
To the lonely sea and the sky,
And all I ask is a tall ship and a star
To steer her by.

John Masefield

⚘

April hath put a spirit of youth in every thing.

William Shakespeare

⚘

Spring is God's way of saying, "One more time!"

Robert Orben

⚘

And God saw every thing that he had made, and, behold, it
was very good.

Genesis 1:31

·Four·

Faith

*O*ne of my favorite places is the little Swiss village of Burgenstock, near Lucerne. It is such a charming mixture of farms, cottages, shops, and hotels that it captures the essence of Swiss beauty and efficiency.

Burgenstock is pervaded by the spirit of a remarkable man named Friedrich Frey, who developed it. Born a peasant, Frey became an important figure in the Swiss power industry and then one of the greatest hotelkeepers in the world. His son Fritz once surprised me with the statement that his father's greatness arose out of a youthful sickness that required him to spend a year in the hospital. When I asked Fritz how that experience led to greatness, he said, "During that year my father read the Bible six times."

From that, Fritz said, his father developed such a faith that, if he were to walk a ridge with steep precipices on both sides, he would do it absolutely without fear: "He was never afraid of anything after the time he poured the Bible down inside himself."

For me, faith is another word for positive thinking. When real faith grips you, you develop a mind-set that looks for the best in everything, refuses to give up, finds a way around (or through) every obstacle, and presses on to victory. Such faith is the consequence of "pouring down inside yourself" the great truths of the Bible and thus being triumphant in human experience.

The quotations in this section, as you make them a vital part of your thoughts and actions, will help you to live positively and triumphantly.

Every day affirm: I am never alone. I can do my job well.
With God's help I can succeed. I am a positive thinker
and believer.

John Glossinger

᛭

Every morning I spend fifteen minutes filling my mind full
of God; and so there's no room left for worry thoughts.

Howard Chandler Christy

᛭

Before me, even as behind,
God is, and all is well.

John Greenleaf Whittier

᛭

I learned really to practice mustard seed faith, and positive
thinking, and remarkable things happened.

Sir John Walton

᛭

Be still, and know that I am God.

Psalm 46:10

᛭

We have grasped the mystery of the atom and rejected the
Sermon on the Mount.

Omar N. Bradley

Now you just believe. That is all you have to do; just believe.

Advice from an old Ohio farmer

Think of only three things—your God, your family, and the Green Bay Packers—in that order.

Vince Lombardi, to his team

Boys, this is only a game. But it's like life in that you will be dealt some bad hands. Take each hand, good or bad, and don't whine and complain but play it out. If you're men enough to do that, God will help and you will come out well.

Dwight D. Eisenhower, quoting his mother

Fear knocked at the door.
Faith answered.
No one was there.

Old saying

If God be for us, who can be against us?

Romans 8:31

The light of God surrounds me,
The love of God enfolds me,
The power of God protects me,
The Presence of God watches over me,
Whatever I am, God is.

Prayer Card

God asks no man whether he will accept life. This is not the choice. You must take it. The only question is how.

Henry Ward Beecher

I am full-fed and yet I hunger. What means this deeper hunger in my heart?

Alfred Noyes

We have only to believe, then little by little we shall see the universal horror unbend and then smile upon us.

Pierre Teilhard De Chardin

Let nothing disturb you, let nothing frighten you: everything passes away except God; God alone is sufficient.

St. Theresa

The Bible tells us that a sparrow does not fall without God's notice. I know he will help us meet our responsibilities through his guidance.

Michael Cardone, Sr.

Faith is the substance of things hoped for, the evidence of things not seen.

Hebrews 11:1

The writers against religion, whilst they oppose every system, are wisely careful never to set up any of their own.

Edmund Burke

The first and finest lesson that parents can teach their children is faith and courage.

Smiley Blanton, M.D.

God gives us always strength enough, and sense enough, for every thing he wants us to do.

John Ruskin

In God we trust.

Motto on U.S. currency

·Five·

Prayer

There are three principal ways to get what we need: by work, by thought, and by prayer. Most people work hard, and some utilize the power of thought. But prayer is greatly neglected. And this is unfortunate, for the most powerful energy one can generate is prayer energy.

How does a person acquire this energy? The first step is simply to pray. As a young man, I was interested in public speaking and listened to some of the greatest orators of my time. Once, after a particularly rousing masterpiece of elocution, I asked the speaker how one could become proficient in that art. His answer was, "By speaking." He explained: "Learn by doing. Speak every time you get a chance. Keep doing it. Practice constantly, seeking to improve your ability."

The best way to learn anything is by doing.

If you want to utilize the matchless power of prayer, begin praying immediately and continue at every opportunity. I have observed from a number of inquiries that the average person probably spends about five minutes a day in prayer. That is one half of 1 percent of one's waking hours. Back in the days of Prohibition in the United States, half of 1 percent of alcohol was declared by act of Congress to be nonintoxicating. That percentage is also nonintoxicating in religion! If you want to experience the heady energy of prayer, practice it more often.

The physician Alexis Carrel, a spiritual pioneer, advised praying everywhere: in the street, the office, the shop, the school. You can transform spare moments by praying for your needs, for those around you, for your friends and loved ones, for everyone and everything you can think of. Then believe that your prayers will be answered. They will be. And prayer is always answered in one of three ways: no, yes, or wait awhile.

Prayer begins where human capacity ends.

Marian Anderson

Work as if you were to live 100 years; pray as if you were to die tomorrow.

Benjamin Franklin

Prayer may not change things for you, but it for sure changes you for things.

Samuel M. Shoemaker

Visualize, "prayerize," "actionize," and your wishes will come true.

Charles L. Allen

When we pray we link ourselves with an inexhaustible motive power.

Alexis Carrel

God listens to our weeping when the occasion itself is beyond our knowledge but still within his love and power.

Daniel A. Poling

Lord, I shall be very busy this day. I may forget thee, but do not thou forget me.

Sir Jacob Astley

What things soever ye desire, when ye pray, believe that ye receive them, and ye shall have them.

Mark 11:24

There are three answers to prayer: yes, no, and wait awhile. It must be recognized that no is an answer.

Ruth Stafford Peale

When I have a problem I pray about it, and what comes to mind and stays there I assume to be my answer. And this has been right so often that I know it is God's answer.

J.L. Kraft

Prayer is a cry of distress, a demand for help, a hymn of love.

Alexis Carrel

Ye have not, because ye ask not.

James 4:2

·Six·
Relationships

$\mathcal{W}$e hear so much about relationships today that one might get the idea that this is a twentieth-century concept. Actually, the importance of good relationships has been known throughout history.

The great Rabbi Hillel (30 B.C.—A.D. 10) was once asked if he could sum up the Jewish law while standing on one foot. He answered: "Do not unto others that which you would not have them do unto you. That is the entire Torah; the rest is commentary." And the ancient law codes of Babylon and China revolve primarily around just and fair relationships.

But our relationships with other people remain today one of our greatest problems. The president of a large company once told me that the most important thing in his business was the relationships among the employees.

During one of Billy Graham's evangelistic crusades in London, the British newspapers quoted some cutting remarks about him by a well-known clergyman of that country. It was reported that when someone began telling Billy about this, he said: "God bless that man. If I were in his place, I'd probably feel the same way about me." Such an attitude ensures personal peace of mind as well as the love and respect of other people.

Mahatma Gandhi spent his whole life helping his fellow citizens achieve their independence. What it took George Washington seven years of bloody war to accomplish, Gandhi did over more than thirty years by the power of quiet, loving nonresistance.

Jesus made it clear that the most important thing in the world is our relationship to God and to others. When we achieve that, everything good will follow.

There can be no daily democracy without daily citizenship.

Ralph Nader

Nothing is ever lost by courtesy. It is the cheapest of pleasures, costs nothing, and conveys much. It pleases him who gives and receives and thus, like mercy, is twice blessed.

Erastus Wiman

Do things for others and you'll find your self-consciousness evaporating like morning dew on a Missouri cornfield in July.

Dale Carnegie

Once a word has been allowed to escape, it cannot be recalled.

Horace

Conscience is the perfect interpreter of life.

Karl Barth

We secure our friends not by accepting favors but by doing them.

Thucydides

Example is not the main thing in influencing others. It is the only thing.

Albert Schweitzer

There is no happiness in having or in getting, but only in giving.

Henry Drummond

Trust not him with your secrets, who left alone in your room, turns over your papers.

Johann Kasper Lavater

Too many people do not care what happens as long as it does not happen to them.

William Howard Taft

Grant that we may not so much seek to be understood as to understand.

St. Francis of Assisi

The shifts of fortune test the reliability of friends.

Marcus Tullius Cicero

Hatred stirreth up strifes: but love covereth all sins.

Proverbs 10:12

You give but little when you give of your possessions. It is when you give of yourself that you truly give.

Kahlil Gibran

You can make more friends in two months by becoming more interested in other people than you can in two years by trying to get people interested in you.

Dale Carnegie

We should behave to our friends as we would wish our friends to behave to us.

Aristotle

What you do not want done to yourself, do not do to others.

Confucius

It is in the character of very few men to honor without envy a friend who has prospered.

Aeschylus

Do all the good you can,
By all the means you can,
In all the ways you can,
In all the places you can,
At all the times you can,
To all the people you can,
As long as ever you can.

John Wesley

This above all: to thine own self be true;
And it must follow, as the night the day,
Thou canst not then be false to any man.

William Shakespeare

·Seven·

Self

Although most of us probably attribute our problems to other people or to bad luck or to the circumstances around us, the truth is that we create our own success or failure. The road to successful, positive living begins with an analysis of ourselves and depends ultimately on how we think of ourselves.

Years ago I wrote: "Without a humble but reasonable confidence in your own powers you cannot succeed. But with sound self-confidence you can succeed. A sense of inferiority and inadequacy interferes with the attainment of your hopes, but self-confidence leads to self-realization and successful achievement" (The Power of Positive Thinking). Now, more than ever, I am convinced that this is true.

How do you build confidence in yourself? Take your mind off the things that seem to be against you. Thinking about negative factors simply builds them up into a power they need not have. Instead, mentally affirm and reaffirm and visualize your assets—the love of God your Father, the ability of your mind and talents, the goodwill of your friends and family, your physical health, your strengths, your future, your possibilities. Stamp indelibly on your mind a picture of yourself succeeding. Make an accurate estimate of your ability, then raise it 10 percent. Affirm that God is with you. Put yourself in his hands and believe that you are now receiving power from him for all your needs.

Read the statements that follow and make them part of yourself. You will learn how to better control your thought processes and, ultimately, your destiny.

I am somebody. I am me. I like being me. And I need
nobody to make me somebody.

Louis L'Amour

I am fearfully and wonderfully made.

Psalm 139:14

Our self-image strongly held essentially determines what
we become.

Maxwell Maltz

I am the master of my fate; I am the captain of my soul.

William Ernest Henley

Self-trust is the first secret of success.

Ralph Waldo Emerson

To go against one's conscience is neither safe nor right.
Here I stand. I cannot do otherwise.

Martin Luther

What a man thinks of himself, that it is which determines or rather indicates his fate.

Henry David Thoreau

Sit loosely in the saddle of life.

Robert Louis Stevenson

Never build a case against yourself.

Robert Rowbottom

Keep strong if possible; in any case keep cool.

Sir Basil Liddell Hart

Adversity causes some men to break; others to break records.

William A. Ward

We are what we believe we are.

Benjamin N. Cardozo

Most people don't plan to fail; they fail to plan.

John L. Beckley

He got the better of himself, and that's the best kind of victory one can wish for.

Miguel De Cervantes

A man can stand a lot as long as he can stand himself.

Axel Munthe

All the resources we need are in the mind.

Theodore Roosevelt, Jr.

Alas! the fearful unbelief is unbelief in yourself.

Thomas Carlyle

Nothing can bring you peace but yourself.

Ralph Waldo Emerson

When people are bored it is primarily with their own selves that they are bored.

Eric Hoffer

It isn't life that matters; it's the courage you bring to it.

Hugh Walpole

The secret to success in life is for a man to be ready for his opportunity when it comes.

Benjamin Disraeli

We're all born under the same sky, but we don't all have the same horizon.

Konrad Adenauer

The good things of life are not to be had singly but come to us with a mixture.

Charles Lamb

Genius is nothing but a greater aptitude for patience.

Benjamin Franklin

Blessed is the man who, having nothing to say, abstains from giving in words evidence of the fact.

George Eliot

The longest journey is the journey inward.

Dag Hammarskjöld

·Eight·

Physical Health

A few years ago, I clipped out a newspaper story about James A. Hard, who lived to the age of one hundred and eleven. One way this man cooperated with the forces of health and longevity, according to the paper, was by taking everything in stride. His friends said he was always happy. He never let himself get overly excited or upset, and he kept control of his life.

At the age of ninety, Mr. Hard had a cataract on one eye. His granddaughter said, "We were going to arrange to have an operation, but Grandpa beat us to it. All by himself, he went to a physician's office where he made the doctor perform the operation. Right after, he came home by himself in a cab. That was nothing but grit and courage."

Emotional tranquility, refusal to worry, the attitude of happiness, zest for life, keeping control, having grit and courage—these are important factors in physical health and long life.

Dr. Bernie S. Siegel of New Haven, Connecticut, believes, as many other physicians do today, that there is a close connection between health and mental attitudes. He sometimes asks his patients, "Why do you need this disease?" When they change their outlook, he reports, their health problems often end.

To practice the basic principles of good health, visualize yourself as sound, healthy and filled with the vitality and boundless life of your Creator. Look upon yourself as the unique individual that you are. Get in harmony with the creative, life-giving, health-maintaining forces of the universe. Affirm peace, wholeness, and good health—and they will be yours.

To get the body in tone, get the mind in tune.

Zachary T. Bercovitz, M.D.

A clean engine always delivers power.

Gas station sign

You can become strongest in your weakest place.

Anonymous Contemporary

The reason worry kills more people than work is that more people worry than work.

Robert Frost

Most of man's trouble comes from his inability to be still.

Blaise Pascal

If you go long enough without a bath even the fleas will let you alone.

Ernie Pyle

A well-spent day brings happy sleep.

Leonardo Da Vinci

Early to bed and early to rise, makes a man healthy, wealthy and wise.

Benjamin Franklin

If you have arthritis, calmly say, "Okay, I have arthritis and this is the way arthritis is." Take pain, like people, as it comes and you can better master it.

Charles Clifford Peale

Hate and fear can poison the body as surely as any toxic chemicals.

Joseph Krimsky, M.D.

Many of my patients could have healthy hearts by just practicing the therapy of their religion.

Louis F. Bishop, M.D.

A merry heart doeth good like a medicine.

Proverbs 17:22

Worry affects the circulation, the heart, the glands, the whole nervous system, and profoundly affects heart action.

Charles W. Mayo, M.D.

The best and most efficient pharmacy is within your own system.

Robert C. Peale, M.D.

Most of the time we think we're sick it's all in the mind.

Thomas Wolfe

Have you that gray sickness—half awake, half asleep—half alive, half dead?

Advertisement caption

I don't know why we are in such a hurry to get up when we fall down. You might think we would lie there and rest awhile.

Max Eastman

The best doctors in the world are Doctor Diet, Doctor Quiet, and Dr. Merryman.

Jonathan Swift

The tongue of the wise is health.

Proverbs 12:18

I am searching for that which every man seeks—
peace and rest.

Dante Alighieri

Do not worry, eat three square meals a day,
say your prayers, be courteous to your creditors,
keep your digestion good, exercise, go slow and easy.

Abraham Lincoln

·Nine·

Mental Health

$\mathcal{A}$t the bottom of the Great Depression of the 1930s I did a lot of counseling, trying to help many troubled people. As I attempted to meet the flood of need, I became aware of the role of unhealthy thought patterns in so many human problems. But I also realized my limitations in psychiatric knowledge, and I began searching for assistance in this important area.

In 1935, I met Dr. Smiley Blanton, one of the finest people I have ever known, skilled in spiritual as well as psychiatric wisdom and sensitivity. After I had told him of my search, Dr. Blanton surprised me by asking, "Do you believe in prayer?" When I assured him that I did, he said, "So do I," explaining that he had been praying for years that he would meet a pastor with whom he could work as a partner, uniting pastoral care with psychological science.

We formed such a team. At first, he counseled me about my problem cases. But he himself became increasingly involved, eventually bringing in young student psychiatrists to work with him. This work finally grew into the Institutes of Religion and Health, which now provide superior accredited training in pastoral counseling. Out of the institutes have developed more than a hundred pastoral counseling centers across the United States.

There is no doubt in my mind that mental and spiritual health are the foundation of physical health, harmonious relationships, and a happy and successful life. The quotations in this book may be thought of as prescriptions. Take one or more a day for increased courage and self-confidence.

Every day give yourself a good mental shampoo.

Sara Jordan, M.D.

The mind is its own place, and in itself can make a heaven of hell, a hell of heaven.

John Milton

Anxiety is the great modern plague. But faith can cure it.

Smiley Blanton, M.D.

Nothing is so much to be feared as fear.

Henry David Thoreau

If you want to conquer fear, don't sit at home and think about it. Go out and get busy.

Dale Carnegie

And be not conformed to this world: but be ye transformed by the renewing of your mind.

Romans 12:2

I know only that what is moral is what you feel good after and what is immoral is what you feel bad after.

Ernest Hemingway

Let us be of good cheer, however, remembering that the misfortunes hardest to bear are those which never come.

James Russell Lowell

Great men are they who see that the spiritual is stronger than any material force; that thoughts rule the world.

Ralph Waldo Emerson

Quiet minds cannot be perplexed or frightened but go on in fortune or misfortune at their own private pace like the ticking of a clock during a thunderstorm.

Robert Louis Stevenson

Positive thinking is the key to success in business, education, pro football, anything that you can mention. I go out there thinking that I am going to complete every pass.

Ron Jaworski

The mind is never right but when it is at peace within itself.

Lucius Annaeus Seneca

Ten

Pain and Suffering

*P*ain and suffering have wracked humanity through-out history. Evidence of arthritis has been discovered in the earliest skeletons of the past.

My friend Lloyd Ogilvie, distinguished pastor of the First Presbyterian Church of Hollywood, California, once said that he had learned several important lessons from personally experiencing pain and suffering. He found he grew the most spiritually during those ordeals. Another lesson was that, on looking back on such an experience afterward, he discovered it had deepened his trust in God. As a result, says Dr. Ogilvie, he is now able to thank God in advance for the prospect of such trials, praying, in effect, "Lord, thank you for the good that is going to happen in and through me as a result of what I am about to experience."

No one welcomes pain. But, rightly faced, it can bring about great good. And we can triumph over it. The day before the January 1988 Superbowl football game, Doug Williams, quarterback for the Washington Redskins, had to endure hours of dental surgery. During the game, his knee was injured. But he led the Redskins to victory in spite of his problems, breaking one record after another. No wonder he was named most valuable player that year!

When pain strikes, we often ask the wrong questions, such as, Why me? The right questions are, What can I learn from this? What can I do about it? What can I accomplish in spite of it?

Bring pain and suffering to the One who suffered for us on a cross and you will find "what a friend we have in Jesus."

One cannot get through life without pain. What we can do is choose how to use the pain life presents to us.

Bernie S. Siegel, M.D.

Is any among you afflicted? Let him pray.

James 5:13

When pain is to be borne, a little courage helps more than much knowledge, a little human sympathy more than much courage, and the least tincture of the love of God more than all.

C.S. Lewis

The pain of the mind is worse than the pain of the body.

Publilius Syrus

He said unto me, My grace is sufficient for thee: for my strength is made perfect in weakness.

2 Corinthians 12:9

And God shall wipe away all tears from their eyes; and there shall be no more death, neither sorrow, nor crying,

neither shall there be any more pain: for the former things
are passed away.

Revelation 21:4

⚬⚬

Diseases can be our spiritual flat tires—disruptions in our
lives that seem to be disasters at the time but end by
redirecting our lives in a meaningful way.

Bernie S. Siegel, M.D.

⚬⚬

In times like these, it helps to recall that there have always
been times like these.

Paul Harvey

⚬⚬

The God of all grace...after that ye have suffered a while,
make you perfect, stablish, strengthen, settle you.

1 Peter 5:10

⚬⚬

Weeping may endure for a night, but joy cometh in
the morning.

Psalm 30:5

·Eleven·

Healing

$\mathcal{W}$hile I was completing this book I met a friend whose son has been plagued by severe emotional problems. "Last Sunday," my friend said, "my son asked me to go to a church that helps him feel better. As soon as I went in, I looked around with interest because there were so many young people present. Some of them were playing drums and guitars and other instruments. The music had a fast beat that I don't usually associate with church. But it was lively, and nearly everyone present was singing and either clapping or raising their hands.

"During a prayer," my friend went on, "the pastor said, 'Lord, we renounce defeat. We renounce poverty. We renounce sickness. We claim health and prosperity and victory in the name of Jesus.' Then the pastor announced some answers to prayer, and people clapped. A woman stood up and said that she wanted to thank those who had been praying about the growth on her kidney. The preceding Tuesday, she said, she had got the results of a CAT scan; the growth had disappeared.

"I guess I'm fussy," my friend concluded, "because some of that isn't my cup of tea. But I wish more churches had that kind of faith and enthusiasm and positive outlook. If they did, there would probably be a lot more people in church."

The encouraging thing is that many churches today seem to be discovering anew the power of positive faith and the reality of healing. Many sick people came to Jesus long ago, and the Gospels tell us "he healed them all." Whether through the science of medicine or the force of faith, God is still healing spirits, minds, and bodies.

Our Creator has given us five senses to help us survive threats from the external world, and a sixth sense, our healing system, to help us survive internal threats.

Bernie S. Siegel, M.D.

❖

What wound did ever heal but by degrees?

William Shakespeare

❖

And the leaves of the tree were for the healing of the nations.

Revelation 22:2

❖

He healeth those that are broken in heart: and giveth medicine to heal their sickness.

The Book of Common Prayer

❖

Health and cheerfulness mutually beget each other.

Joseph Addison

❖

The first petition that we are to make to Almighty God is for a good conscience, the next for health of mind, and then of body.

Lucius Annaeus Seneca

To wish to be well is a part of becoming well.

Lucius Annaeus Seneca

⁂

I shall yet praise him, who is the health of my countenance, and my God.

Psalm 42:11

⁂

Sometimes a light surprises
The Christian while he sings;
It is the Lord who rises
With healing in his wings.

William Cowper

⁂

Sleep that knits up the ravell'd sleave of care,
The death of each day's life, sore labor's bath,
Balm of hurt minds, great nature's second course,
Chief nourisher in life's feast.

William Shakespeare

⁂

Jesus Christ maketh thee whole.

Acts 9:34

·Twelve·

Community

The ancient words, "It is not good that the man should be alone" (Genesis 2:18), apply to more than love and marriage. Modern science is replete with evidence that it is good for human beings to live in community, to relate constructively to others in various ways, from local groups to patriotic endeavors and worldwide ventures in brotherhood and sisterhood.

While I was an active pastor, I supported ecumenical efforts and councils of churches. At one gathering of the New York City Council of Churches, of which I was once president, I remarked that if no such organization existed, someone would have had to invent it, so important is its work. I have long been active in Rotary and similar organizations where there is not only camaraderie but participation in projects of goodwill.

And I am an enthusiastic citizen of the United States of America. This country's great heritage of freedom comes from the mingling of two mighty streams. One stream is that of classical antiquity. The great thinkers of ancient Greece held that the human mind is sacred and that no one must enslave it. The other stream is that of the Judeo-Christian heritage, which upholds the infinite worth and the right to freedom of every individual.

It is very interesting that this ideal of freedom is now being sought, and often celebrated, in almost every country on earth. For the idea of community cannot be satisfied until it embraces the whole world. The ancient prophets and mystics had a noble vision of worldwide human kinship and peace. As we reach out positively to others, each one of us can bring that vision closer to reality.

Learn to do well; seek judgment, relieve the oppressed, judge the fatherless, plead for the widow.

Isaiah 1:17

Man's inhumanity to man makes countless thousands mourn.

Robert Burns

Those who corrupt the public mind are just as evil as those who steal from the public purse.

Adlai Stevenson

Rebellion to tyrants is obedience to God.

Thomas Jefferson

Heaven is above all yet; there sits a judge
That no king can corrupt.

William Shakespeare

Oh, what times! Oh, what standards!

Marcus Tullius Cicero

Where there is no vision, the people perish: but he that keepeth the law, happy is he.

Proverbs 29:18

We shall overcome, we shall overcome
We shall overcome someday
Oh, deep in my heart, I do believe
We shall overcome someday.

Civil Rights Song

Who, then, is free? The wise man who can govern himself.

Horace

Nothing emboldens sin so much as mercy.

William Shakespeare

Whither is fled the visionary gleam
Where is it now, the glory and the dream?

William Wordsworth

Blessed are the peacemakers.

Matthew 5:9

I pray heaven to bestow the best of all blessings on this house and all that hereafter shall inhabit it. May none but honest and wise men ever rule under this roof.

John Adams, Inscription in White House

I decline to accept the end of man.

William Faulkner

Unfortunately, many Americans live on the outskirts of hope—some because of their poverty, some because of their color, and all too many because of both. Our task is to help replace their despair with opportunity.

Lyndon Baines Johnson

We are confronted primarily with a moral issue. It is as old as the Scriptures and is as clear as the American Constitution.

John F. Kennedy

Injustice anywhere is a threat to justice everywhere.

Martin Luther King, Jr.

The God who gave us life gave us liberty at the same time.

Thomas Jefferson

This will remain the land of the free only so long as it is the land of the brave.

Elmer Davis

Either war is obsolete or men are.

R. Buckminster Fuller

·Thirteen·

Love and Family

Family trees are interesting. My mother's father, Andrew DeLaney, was born in Ballynakill, Ireland. But as a lad he stowed away on a ship bound for America, where he married blue-eyed Margaret Potts and became an industrious Ohioan. My mother, Anna DeLaney, had a face matched by the beauty of her character. A hard worker, she took a happy delight in life and possessed the gift of infectious laughter.

The Peales came from England; my great grandfather Thomas Peale was one of the early settlers of Lynchburg, Ohio. His sons Samuel and Wilson Peale operated a dry goods store. My father, Charles Clifford Peale, was trained as a physician and, after practicing medicine for some time, became a full-time minister. As both an M.D. and a D.D., Father sometimes punned whimsically that he was a "pair-o'-docs." Father was one of the first men to demonstrate the partnership of spiritual with physical health.

My wife Ruth's parents were Canadians. Her father, Frank Burton Stafford, was a minister, one of the finest men I have ever known. Her mother, Loretta Crosby Stafford, combined a saintly character with strength and firmness.

The dynamic qualities of enthusiasm, excitement, energy, and faith run like golden cords through the lives of the Staffords, the Peales, the Crosbys, and the DeLaneys. And they manifest themselves in each of our children—Margaret, John, and Elizabeth—and their spouses and children. How fortunate I am to be part of such a splendid family.

Families, like individuals, are unique. Cherish your family connections. They are one of God's greatest ways of demonstrating his love and fellowship.

Love is a gentle courtesy.

Anonymous

There are three faithful friends—an old wife, an old dog, and ready money.

Benjamin Franklin

There is no more lovely, friendly, and charming relationship, communion, or company than a good marriage.

Martin Luther

One's best asset is a sympathetic spouse.

Euripides

Love yields to business. If you seek a way out of love, be busy; you'll be safe then.

Ovid

'Tis better to have loved and lost
Than never to have loved at all.

Alfred Lord Tennyson

I speak Spanish to God, Italian to women, French to men, and German to my horse.

Charles V of France

⁕

Her voice is full of money.

Anonymous

⁕

Absence makes the heart grow fonder.

Sextus Aurelius Propertius

⁕

The heart has reasons which the reason cannot understand.

Blaise Pascal

·Fourteen·

Aging

$\mathcal{T}$ he process of aging is often thought of as a slow, sad descent into the grave. I suppose I am fortunate in having been exposed all my life to dynamic men and women who lived to a vigorous old age and whose passing from this life seemed not a defeat but a celebration. My parents, my wife's parents, and many of our ancestors lived considerably beyond the traditional "threescore years and ten." And I have often been impressed by people who displayed uncommon energy and good health into their seventies, eighties, and nineties.

One such person was William H. Danforth, head of the Ralston Purina Company, who, as a sickly child, accepted his teacher's dare to become the healthiest boy in his class. He not only did so but inspired thousands of others to be their best both physically and spiritually with his book *I Dare You.* In his "old age," Danforth was an amazing example of tireless energy. So was the vaudeville entertainer Mort Cheshire, who still played the "bones" vigorously at the age of one hundred and two.

Nearly forty years ago, I wrote in *The Power of Positive Thinking,* "The longer I live the more I am convinced that neither age nor circumstance need to deprive us of energy and vitality." I still find that true. Although I have retired from my church, I occupy my working hours with *Guideposts* magazine, the Foundation for Christian Living, speaking, and writing books and articles. I go to bed as early as possible every night, usually sleep soundly and rise early. I try to eat sensibly, exercise regularly, and avoid bad habits of all kinds.

I mentally repudiate physical, mental, or spiritual decline or disability. I trust in the living God. And I recommend the same to anyone who desires a long and healthy life.

Live your life and forget your age.

Frank Bering

Never think any oldish thoughts. It's oldish thoughts that make a person old.

James A. Farley

Don't look back. Something may be gaining on you.

Satchel Paige

Little by little the time goes by,
Short if you sing it, long if you sigh.

Anonymous

I dare you to be healthy, live a long time, and never think old age.

William H. Danforth

It is wonderful to be young, but it is equally desirable to be mature and rich in experience.

Bernard Baruch

I am not interested in the past. I am interested in the future, for that is where I expect to spend the rest of my life.

Charles F. Kettering

If wrinkles must be written upon our brows, let them not be written upon the heart. The spirit should not grow old.

James A. Garfield

None are so old as those who have outlived enthusiasm.

Henry David Thoreau

He who is of a calm and happy nature will hardly feel the pressure of age.

Plato

To know how to grow old is the master-work of wisdom, and one of the most difficult chapters in the great art of living.

Henri Frederic Amiel

If you carry your childhood with you, you never become older.

Abraham Sutzkever

A man's life is what his thoughts make of it.

Marcus Aurelius

We may let go all things which we cannot carry into the eternal life.

Anna R. Brown Lindsay

When life was like a story, holding neither sob nor sigh
In the golden olden glory of the days gone by.

James Whitcomb Riley

If you wait for the perfect moment when all is safe and assured, it may never arrive. Mountains will not be climbed, races won, or lasting happiness achieved.

Maurice Chevalier

Give me a young man in whom there is something of the old, and an old man in whom there is something of the young. Guided so, a man may grow old in body but never in mind.

Marcus Tullius Cicero

So teach us to number our days, that we may apply our hearts unto wisdom.

Psalm 90:12

It is always in season for old men to learn.

Aeschylus

The hoary head is a crown of glory.

Proverbs 16:31

For of all sad words of tongues or pen
The saddest are these: It might have been.

John Greenleaf Whittier

Time's wheel runs back or stops: Potter and clay endure.

Robert Browning

The future is something which everyone reaches at the rate of sixty minutes an hour, whatever he does, whoever he is.

C.S. Lewis

·Fifteen·

Death and Beyond

What we call death comes eventually to every one of us. And the loss of a loved one is usually a heart-rending experience.

Early in my ministry, I noticed a black wreath on a door in my city parish. It was the Christmas season. I did not know anyone at the address, but I knocked on the door and discovered that a little girl had died. When I saw that beautiful child in her casket, I wanted to hold the parents in my arms and weep with them. I could hardly find words to express my feelings. But the bereaved father and mother must have felt my grief, for what I did say seemed to give them some comfort.

One of my lifelong convictions is that death, far from being the end, is but the door to an existence larger and more glorious than any human conception. Years ago, my wife, Ruth, and I took a helicopter ride above the Swiss Alps. Leaving the heliport at Zermatt, we flew up a green valley and doubled back over the little toy village far below. Then we soared past the peaks of Gornergrat and Stockhorn and over a vast gleaming glacier.

But suddenly the glacier came to an abrupt end. We hung suspended over what seemed to be *nothing*. We were at least eleven thousand feet high—and it seemed as though there was only an empty void below. Later Ruth wrote about that flight, "Perhaps dying is like that: an outward rush into the unknown where there is nothing recognizable, nothing to cling to, and yet you are sustained and supported over the great void just as you were over the comfortable and familiar terrain."

Helen Steiner Rice once wrote, "The end of the road is but a bend in the road." I believe that is true of life and death. At the end of God's world there is his endless world beyond.

As a well-spent day brings happy sleep, so life well used brings happy death.

Leonardo Da Vinci

When a man dies, if he can pass enthusiasm along to his children, he has left them an estate of incalculable value.

Thomas A. Edison

In the night of death hope sees a star and listening love can hear the rustle of a wing.

Robert Ingersoll

Peace I leave with you, my peace I give unto you: not as the world giveth, give I unto you.

John 14:27

We are citizens of eternity.

Feodor Dostoevski

When the one Great Scorer comes to write against your name, he marks not that you won or lost, but how you played the game.

Grantland Rice

Pale death with impartial tread beats at the poor man's cottage door and at the palaces of kings.

Horace

It is well. I die hard but I am not afraid to go.

George Washington

Though I walk through the valley of the shadow of death, I will fear no evil: for thou art with me.

Psalm 23:4

We do not believe in immortality because we can prove it, but we try to prove it because we cannot help believing it.

Harriet Martineau

No man is an island, entire of itself; every man is a piece of the continent, a part of the main. If a clod be washed away by the sea, Europe is the less, as well as if a promontory were, as well as if a manor of thy friend's or of thine own were. Any man's death diminishes me because I am involved in mankind; and therefore never send to know for whom the bell tolls; it tolls for thee.

John Donne

Designed by Robert J. Pantelone
Edited by Stephanie Oda
Type set in Usherwood Book and Diskus